AF226121

May we never lose our childlike imagination

Mr. germ in the eyes of a child

Illustrated by Kelcy Curtsinger

Mr. Germ

Written by Jacki Elam

Illustrated by Brian Ashby

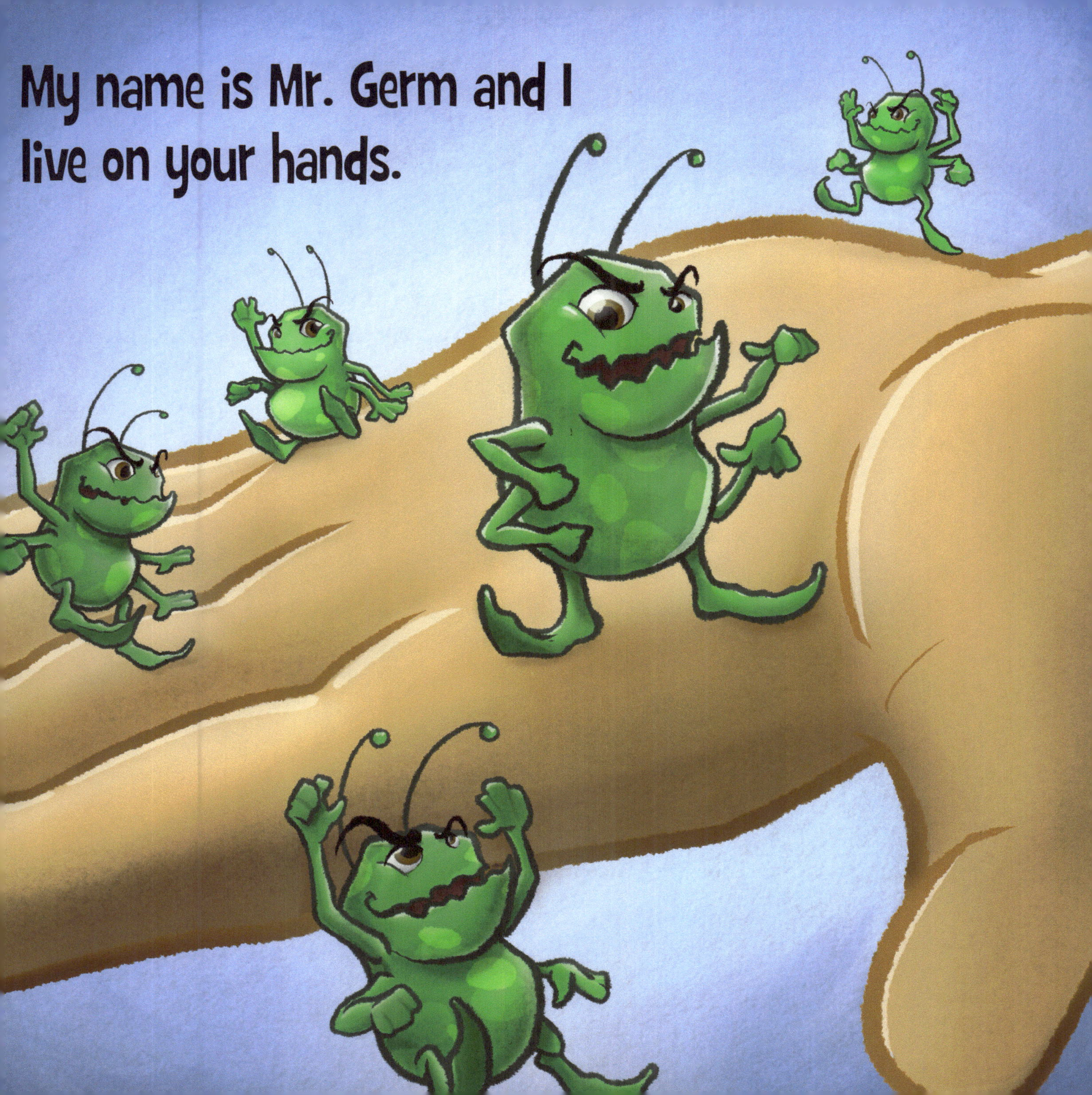

My name is Mr. Germ and I
live on your hands.

I wanna
take you
home
and
finish
out my
plans.

I wanna make you sick,
see, that's what I do.

I go from place to place
spreading my goo.

But first, don't let me fail with the introduction
of my friends on the trail of illness induction!

Don't forget about me,
I'm a virus...

I'm gonna work my way in
and heat your body up like
fireworks!

DANGER
DANGER

Hello my friends I am a fungi here just to say hi...
sliming my way around to ensure your body
temp stays real high! Or just give
ya some really gross feet.

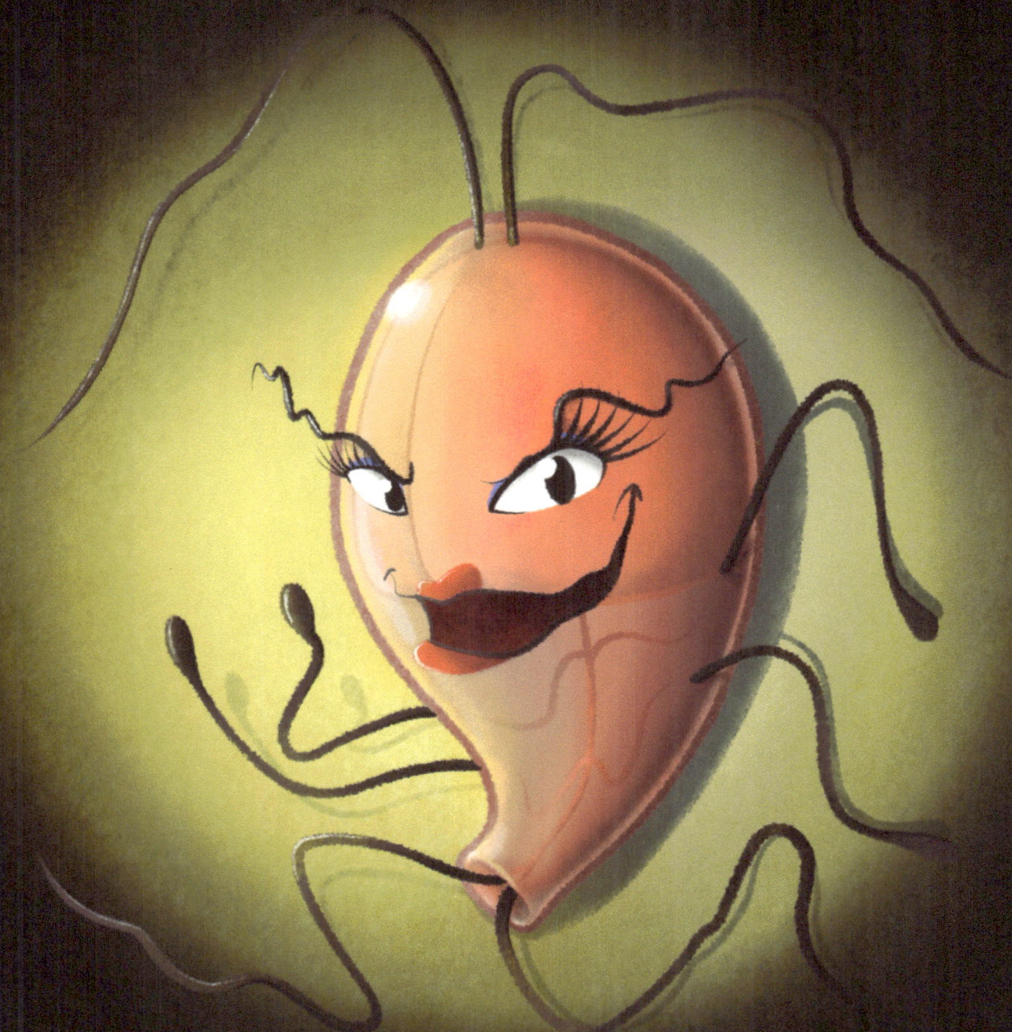

Protozoa? I don't even know ya. I am
rather rare and I thought you should be aware.

If I sneak inside you'll feel like you have
been attacked by a bear.

Well I almost forgot about my special friends because sometimes we are on the outs?!? They tend to get jealous of me because they've got meds to zap them but none that completely demolish me.

That's me, I'm Bacteria. I'll act like I don't even know ya
when you're screaming out in agony from the ills
I can throw ya!

As if my plan couldn't get any better, my villain world has welcomed a new member. A warm welcome to Corona virus aka **COVID-19**. My team just keeps getting more sinister!

Well now they've had their say, but let me stop them right there. I wanna help you fight those bad guys and stop their sneaky, slimy ways!! Nurse Goodbody here to give you the weapons to be a healthy warrior and keep those bad guys at bay!!

So wash those hands and scrub those fingernails. Count until you can't sing happy birthday anymore...well, singing the same ole verse three times ought to do ya good!

Did I say do not touch your face?!?! Well, I meant to and as well, always try to keep your personal space.

Wait, you feel a sneeze coming on and don't have a tissue?

Quick! Use your armpit or your elbow to catch it!

And remember this important fact. After you go potty and then you flush, well, you have to remember your hands need a brush! Time to sing your song again...did you pick a favorite tune?

Got some more important stuff that I think you need to know. Leave your shoes at the door so germs don't track all on the floor no more!

After a week of dragging your backpack through the trenches of germs and stenches.
Baggy
ROCK

You might want to throw it in the wash
with the britches!

Ok now, can you remember these important facts?

I know you love your doggo and your fluffy kitty too but you gotta remember they have germs too!

I don't know about you
but one of my favorite
things to do is to have a
snack or two.

Before you dig in, grab a
hand wipe or go to the loo...
yep, time to get your groove
on and sing that song again!
CHIPS
PIZZA
Cho

Don't drink after others.
BLAAAAH!

Don't share your fork or spoon!

Keep your electronic devices
shining like the moon.

With these important tips you can stay healthy as a bandit.

And have a healthy immune...system that is!!!

And once again don't
touch your face!